C000051002

**A Short Guide
by David Leddick**

BRUNO GMÜNDER

© 2012 Bruno Gmünder Verlag GmbH
Kleiststraße 23-26, D-10787 Berlin
info@brunogmuender.com
© 2011 David Leddick
Photographs: © 2011 David Vance,
except p. 11 © iStockphoto/Lisa Thornberg and
pp. 23 left, 24 and 27 © iStockphoto/pederk
Layout: Steffen Kawelke
Printed in South Korea

ISBN 978-3-86787-383-3

More about our books and authors:
www.brunogmuender.com

Contents

Dear Gay (or Non-Gay) Reader,

When we wake up in the dark we are always seventeen. We lie there accusing ourselves of all sorts of fears and guilts and general inadequacies. Yet in the broad light of day when we consider how we would have dealt with a problem at seventeen and how we would deal with it today, it is quite obvious that we have matured and grown a great deal.

We are in the 21st century. We must grow and mature even more. The world we will be living in will be quite different and all our repressions, hesitations, feelings of not being good enough, fears of being rejected will not be appropriate in this new environment.

Already it is quite clear that the gay world has become very American Butch with all its hockey and volleyball tournaments. I myself will miss all those long and languid lovelies who never played sports. And certainly there are plenty of men still interested in them. The gay image has transmuted from Rita Hayworth through Billie Jean King and now is hovering around Adam Lambert. And so the world changes. "Kismet", as they say, "It is written in the stars."

Your problems can become your lifestyle.
Don't get locked into your problems so they become the way you live. You will have new problems. So be ready to change and live in terms of them. You don't want to be an old fuddy-duddy. And remember:

If there isn't any solution, its not a problem.
It's just a situation. This is what being gay is all about. It's not a problem, it's just a situation called being alive. Here are some things I want you to remember before you continue with this guidebook:

There is nothing wrong with being gay.
Some of the big names in history were gay and liked it fine. Alexander the Great. And so beautiful, too. King Ludwig of Bavaria. Mad as a hatter, but the country is living on the tourist income from his crazy palaces. Frederick the Great. Frederick was great, they say. Richard the Lionhearted. His ex became the King of France.

George Washington. Married late to a widow who already had two children. Never had children of his own. Was crazy about young General Lafayette. President Buchanan. His boyfriend lived with him in the White House. Bet you didn't know that. Even Abraham Lincoln. Who had a great body and was suspected of lurking in the park in front of the White House. More power to him.

Don't feel guilty.
If you don't already know this, you should. The Kinsey Report, published more than half a century ago, stated that 37 per cent of the male white population of the United States had at least some overt homosexual experience to the point of orgasm between adolescence and old age; 23 per cent of the male population had some kind of homosexual experience for at least three years between the ages of 16 and 55. This is a lot of people and this was in the far more repressive American

world of over fifty years ago. Just to point out that you are hardly in this gay thing by yourself. Kinsey's figures for exclusively homosexual males were 4 per cent, which were about four million men then. And would be over ten million guys today. Just to give you some facts so you don't feel lonely.

It is very important not to feel guilty. How? Don't do things that make you feel guilty. If you feel guilty about doing certain things (blowjobs behind garbage cans for example), either face the fact that you actually enjoy suffering the guilt, or just quit doing it. Feeling that you are a bad person is so 20th Century. Get over it. The 21st Century has a whole new set of definitions of being bad: like bombing people, destroying the environment, neglecting the poor and underprivileged. That is being bad. You aren't.

So here's the story. In the century ahead it's going be all about tailoring a life for yourself that suits you and makes you feel fulfilled, and that comes pretty close to being happy. It's not about doing what is expected of you by others or trying to look good in the eyes of others at the expense of your own happiness. That is all over.

And to do this, you have to know who you are. That is the reason for doing this book. Find out who you are and get on with it. With all best wishes for your success,

David Leddick

Get Out of the Closet!

If you are not willing to get out of the closet you might as well close this book right now and read no further. You can not be a successful gay person and be in the closet. You are creating a life for a non-person; the person you would be if you were straight. None of these roles have anything to do with you. And when you lay down to die you will realize that you never really lived. And you will just have to do it all over again. And surely it will be as a gay person. So you might just as well deal with it now.

You can't tell your parents? Then don't. Just move to Seattle or as far away as you can and don't write. And get on with it. Any man over thirty who is not trying to fuck women should think a bit, "Who do I want to fuck?". If you don't date girls and you think most people don't think you're gay, you're kidding yourself. This is the communication age. Everybody knows everything. Everyone is smarter than you think they are.

The trouble with a secret life is that the only person who thinks it's a secret is the person living it. Everyone else knows. So if you think

the shock of your coming out will alienate your friends and family, forget it.

1. If you are not out of the closet you cannot have an honest relationship with another man. Anyone who is worth caring about is not going to want to spend his life meeting you at out-of-town hotels.

2. You are wasting an enormous amount of emotional energy trying to conceal something most people don't care about. The world is like a classroom of children with their heads down on their desks. When you raise your head, you discover there isn't any teacher. You may do as you please. Everyone else has their heads down. They don't care.

3. You are walking around with enormous weight hanging over your head. Imagine how wonderful it would feel to be rid of it.

4. You are not getting on with your life. Life is about living, being happy, finding work you like or money you like, loving some-one madly, badly, and gladly. It's not about big secrets.

5. You may not want to join a gay world that you see as a lot of aging poofs. You are probably afraid that once you're out you will be part of a gay world that is a lot of men wearing pink tutus in a bar somewhere. Hello! And grow up.

The list could go on indefinitely. The number of families in the United States that constitute Mom, Dad and the kids is only about 23% of the population. The bulk of the people in this country are trying to work out lifestyles that suit who they are, not what other people think they should be. Join the mob.

This will be quite a short chapter. You want to live a lie? Please do it on your own. Don't involve innocent women and children.

You will say:

1. I want to have a settled domestic life. You can, darling, but it doesn't have to be next door to your parents in the suburbs. In fact, it can't be. You can have a settled domestic life with a male partner. You can have a settled domestic life with a group of friends. You can have a settled domestic life all by yourself. The idea that you will have no more problems once you are settled in the suburbs with a family is a false one. The troubles are just beginning in fact.

2. I want to have children. Fine. Have them. God knows there are tons of lost kids in orphanages all

over the world. If you feel you must have children that are the fruit of your own loins, you can figure that out with close lesbian friends also. People are doing it all over the country. But to get married to have children who will never

know their Dad is gay? Is that fair? They will never really know you, the real you, and you will never really know them. So what's the point?

What you don't realize is:

1. You will cheat on your wife with truck drivers and then feel horribly guilty.

You will never be able to tell her about your double life and you will never be really intimate with her. And when she finds out, which she will, she will be destroyed and you will have fucked up someone else's life thoroughly. It's not a good feeling. This does not sound like a recipe for happiness.

2. When the kids are grown and out of the house you will find you can no longer deal with not having a man in your life and you will start going to gay bars, meet someone much younger than yourself, leave your wife and try to replicate your married life with a man. This won't work either. You will start doing three ways, four ways and five ways. Your looks will be shot. You will be desperate and settle for anyone as a bed partner. This is not a pretty picture either. However accurate.

My friend, a basic rule for successful gay living in the 21st century is "To thine own self be true." Sorry you had to hear it, but there's no way around it. Heterosexual or homosexual it's not easy finding a life partner, and maybe a life partner isn't even the way to happiness for you. Consider that.

Should You Tell Your Parents?

Please notice this chapter is not entitled "How To Tell Your Parents." I'm not so sure that every parent deserves to hear the good news.

This is perhaps a good place to discuss the traditional American policy of "Don't ask, don't tell", which existed long before President Clinton suggested it for the gays in military service.

The world has an unfortunate tendency to think in prototypical terms. Every marriage is happy, or should be. Every parent loves their child and every child loves his/her parents. Or should. Historically this has never been the case. Where people got the idea in the face of so much evidence otherwise is beyond me. Think of:

Medea. She killed her kids to revenge herself on her husband when he left her for another woman. Orestes. He killed his mother (and her boyfriend) when they did away with Dad. Hamlet. Need we even go into this? His uncle killed his father and immediately Mom married the

killer. Nice. That lady who pushed her car into a lake with the kids in it in Texas. Not very nice.

The list goes on but we always insist that these are the exceptions. There are mucho, mucho exceptions. Keep in mind we don't all necessarily have to have a swell relationship with the folks.

If your parents don't like your being gay maybe they're not very nice people.

Let's face it. Your relationship with your parents can be very much like your relationship with a burned-out lover. Drop them before they drop you. And go find a nice older couple who really like you and would love to have you visit, love to have their birthdays remembered, would love to have you take care of them when they're old.

Get real. Many people marry other people they don't love. Many of those people then have children, by someone they don't particularly love. They don't automatically love that child? Sometimes an unhappily married parent will reject the child who is desperately looking to be loved. As a way of getting even with their spouse.

I have known many people who do not instinctively want to pick up small children, hug them, kiss them, reassure them that everything will be all right. These are bum parents. You may have bum parents. I have just one piece of advice on this. The same piece of advice anyone will offer you about a bum lover. *They will never change.* Don't expect it. Don't wait for it. And for God's sake don't spend a fortune and decades of your life with an analyst hoping it will happen. As I have said before, if there's no solution it isn't a problem. It's just a situation.

And you can just learn to live with it. Like the fact you have no sense of rhythm. When I was your age I lived in New York and hated visiting the family on holidays. (Does this sound familiar?) They never asked anything about my life and insisted that I play the role in the family I always had. (Incompetent younger brother.) My solution?

I pretended they were clients, like ones I had at the advertising agency where I worked, and that I was being paid $1,000 a day to be with them and be entertaining.

My total superficiality worked like a charm. "You're so much easier to get along with!" was the cry. Now there was no request that they stop watching television and talk to me. I no longer tried to discuss how abusive Dad had been. No more exclamations of "Oh you're so emotional!" from them. If you imagine you're being well paid to be with them, time slips right by.

It's all about them, it's not about you.

Most parents don't like your being gay because it embarrasses them. They don't give a hoot in hell about your happiness. You are to be happy on their terms only, so it reflects well upon them. And in typically American terms, what reflects well upon them is that you make a lot of money, you are famous, and you have the requisite little wifey and kids. Over and out.

Is this all too obvious? Have you already had this discussion hur dreds of times with your friends? Well, all I can bring to the party is the conclusion that this is not a problem for which there is a solution. It's only a situation. Leave it alone and forget it.

Of course they also fear, if you are gay *it is all their fault*. They don't want to feel guilty. They want you to feel guilty. That is if they're even focused enough to think about you. My mother kept daily diaries for many years. My brother said as he handed them to me, "Don't worry, you weren't her favorite." I was struck by the fact that she almost never mentioned me. Or any of my siblings unless they were getting divorced, giving birth, or having nervous collapses. Otherwise her diaries were full

of her school teaching day, the garden, the weather. She thought about us amazingly little. This is also undoubtedly true of your own parents.

Shortly before her 80th birthday, my oldest brother asked her, "Mom, what were your happiest years?" She replied, "Oh from 40 to 45. I was working, I had money, I had friends, I traveled a lot."

He said, somewhat stupefied, "It wasn't when we were with you?" My mother, who was not bourgeoise and an honest woman answered, "Oh no. When you were with me all I did was worry." Learn from this. Your parents are only relieved that you are out of the house and didn't die on them en route.

Everything is all right.

This is all your parents want to know. They do not want to be your best friend. They do not want any real intimacy. The idea that intimacy is a family function came out of somewhere but that is not how families really work. Family is where you go when you can't go anywhere else. Your childhood is so rife with psychological drama, trauma, excitement, abuse, emotional ups and downs, isn't it better to just put it on ice and get on with it? I'm sure your parents would agree.

That eccentric English personality Quentin Crisp once told me that as he was leaving the stage door of a theater in Boston a young man rushed up with an older woman in tow and gushed," Oh, Mr. Crisp,

I have so much to thank you for! Seeing your performance gave me the courage to tell my mother I was gay." Quentin replied. "I'm not sure that was a good idea." The mother immediately chimed in, "That's what I told him."

Recommendations:

1. Tell your parents you're gay if you feel like it. The only one it's going to make feel better is you. Just be gay and I assure you that will be quite enough. When they come to visit you and see that Jim and you are sleeping together in the same bed there should be few questions left.

2. Try directing your conversation with your parents towards their relationship. It's probably terrible. Quentin Crisp also told me about riding on a train to the West Coast, seated opposite an elderly lady who offered the information, "My husband just died after fifty years of marriage." As Quentin was about to offer her his sympathies, she added, "And oh, what a relief."

So there you have it:

1. Being intimate with one's parents is something of a fiction. It isn't very common.

2. Their only concern about you being gay is that it reflects poorly on them.

3. There is really nothing to be done about this.

4. Their real concern is themselves, not you, kiddo.

Go ahead. Make your decision. But please try to keep it in perspective. It's not a terrible mistake if you don't tell them. And don't expect some miracle of closeness to occur if you do. Just give them the impression that you are fine, that you are happy. That's all they want to hear. And all you owe them.

Parents are like lovers. Don't try to make someone love you who just isn't going to. And who in fact will try to control you by withholding his/her love. Drop them. Like a hot potato. And go find someone who will love you, wants to love you, and needs to love you, like any decent parent would.

Don't be a Bitch!

Here's the question, where did gay men get the idea that they should style themselves on some 1940s movie star, like Bette Davis or Joan Crawford? There aren't any woman around like that anymore.

The idea that because you are gay you can enter the room with your hand on your hip and say something unkind to every person in the room is old-fashioned. You don't have to lumber in wearing a plaid shirt and a two-day old beard either. All of that stuff is styling yourself on somebody else.

Be yourself. And remember you can be witty without being bitchy. Being bitchy suggests that you have thrown in the towel as far as your own personal aspirations are concerned. You no longer believe in love, you no longer believe other people can be kind and considerate, you no longer believe in being helpful to others. And all the time,

inside you are still hoping that Mr. Right will come along. And see through your sophisticated veneer and take you away from all this. Am I correct? You know I am. Being a bitch suggests you think you are better than other people. You know you're not.

Being a bitch creates an impression that you are invulnerable. You know that you are not. You're just trying to hurt others before they hurt you. This is a childish way to behave.

Being a bitch makes you the center of attention. Everyone laughs with you. And you go home alone.

Being a bitch communicates to any thinking person that you are not very happy with yourself. Do you really want to communicate this?

And most dire of all, being a bitch is old-fashioned. It is part and parcel of that period style of walking as though you are wearing heels and a tight skirt. Of shaking invisible bracelets down your slender wrists. Of standing with one hip out and a languid hand upon it. The glamour girls are all gone.

Being a bitch is part of the package of low self-esteem and lack of self-confidence. You aren't even going to try to be happy and you don't want anyone else to be either. You know this when you see it in other people. Know it in yourself.

So:

1. Don't try to steal your friend's boyfriend.

2. Do not say mean things about other gay men, particularly after you've slept with them.

3. Do not try to get out of paying your share of the dinner check.

4. Buy other people drinks as well as letting them buy yours.

5. Do not shoplift.

6. Do not make fun of other people's bodies.

7. Do not make fun of other people's penises

8. Do not gauge desirability on the size of someone else's penis.

9. Do not sit at home alone drinking or smoking pot thinking that no one likes you. They have every reason not to.

10. Do not be casual about accepting invitations. If you accept, you must go. If you don't want to accept, tell them your dog just died.

Being a bitch is a prototypical heterosexual view of a gay man. Don't give them the ammunition.

You do not want to be a prototype.

Did You Really Have Sex?

This is the sex chapter. The big untold secret about sex is that it varies widely from good sex over a wide spectrum to bad sex, and it isn't always the same for both partners.

Bette Midler used to have a number where she tunelessly sang a kind of folk song about meeting a cute sailor on the street and going back to her room and there they had: "....bad sex, the worst sex I ever had."

Let's face it, sex can be bad. Even if the definition of a bad blowjob is "fabulous." So let's talk about and what can be done about it.

Is it just foreplay?

What many gay men call sex many people would only call foreplay. One of my friends has two definitions for this kind of hasty sexual clash with strangers. "Boy Scout Sex" and "Fast Food Jack Off." That pretty well says it all.

During the Clinton scandal when White House intern Monica Lewinsky crawled under the president's desk, Europeans were very perplexed at the outrage in the USA. A Swedish female reader wrote the International Herald Tribune in Paris about her confusion. "But there was only foreplay!" she said. Evidently President Clinton and she had the same view as to what constitutes sexual intercourse.

My friends, fooling around in the world of foreplay and not going further says something demeaning about one or both parties. As with poor Monica, aren't you enough of a sex object for the other party to want to do the big thing? Don't you think well enough of yourself to want or demand more? Or don't you want to be so intimate as to actually take all your clothes off and "go all the way" as they so sweetly put it in the 1930s.

Do you want sex or do you want notches?

Going to a bar, making off with an attractive stranger, touching each other's private parts to the point that someone has an orgasm, and then returning to the real world

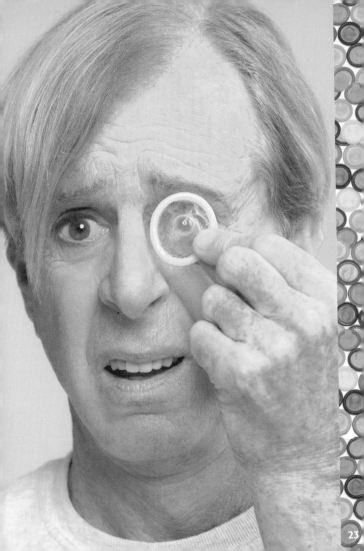

feeling assured that you are still attractive and can still "get" good looking men, is this a sex life? I leave the answer to you.

Do gentlemen prefer strangers?

So what's with this thing about only wanting to have sex with strangers in some obscure location, frequently dangerous? Edmund White wrote in a recent book about wandering around Paris that his best sex was with strangers down along the Seine. Mr. White then wrote a beautiful book about his longtime lover who died of AIDS. Am I not understanding something here? What kind of sex did they have then? It sounds like sexual fulfillment and love fell into two quite separate categories. If the same could be said for you, I think your missing something and you really shouldn't go to your grave without experiencing it.

Does having real sex say too much about you?

I think many men find intercourse embarrassing. You have to really let yourself go to truly enjoy it. And they don't want to go that far. This is our English heritage. "No

Sex Please, We're British." Quentin Crisp wrote in his "How To Have A Lifestyle" that for the English " … to have emotions is embarrassing. To discuss them is disgusting." So you can imagine where that puts having that revelatory activity, sex.

If you have that restrictive feeling about sex, you may have what may be called "poor self image," "low self esteem," "lack of confidence," you name it. You've heard all that stuff. So if you feel bad about being gay, that's an open invitation for having bad sex.

Is this section making you feel really mad? Are you muttering under your breath and saying things like "This guy knows nothing about sex." "He knows nothing about hot sex with truck drivers behind dumpsters alongside the Expressway." "This book is crap." Good. Now we're getting somewhere. You're angry. And anger is always the manifestation of fear. So what are you afraid of?

Have you ever had really good sex?

This is what frightens people, gay men only a small percentage in the overall population. Are they going to go through life and have that feeling that great sex never really happened? One of the finest quotes I ever overheard on the streets of Miami Beach was, "He fucked me so hard my mother came." I believe you only get that excited by someone else in bed when you really know whom you're fucking and that sexual intercourse is bringing you closer together than anything else can. Great sex is when those two miserable little particles of awareness come together and realize, "We're not two little separate things, we're one much bigger thing." And of course you go back to being one little miserable thing, but you can keep re-joining. And even if you can't, you never forget it. Which brings us to love.

Non-gay sex

This is a little aside. No one has ever done any research about heterosexual sex from an enjoyment standpoint. Dr. Alfred Kinsey did the most exhaustive sexual research ever done back in the 1940s and 1950s and the United States still hasn't let it sink in. Particularly that little figure of 37% of the adult men in the United States having had sexual contact with an-

other man after the age of 21. Let's not go there.

How many married couples actually have a thriving and enjoyable sex life? I am not offering any guesses but I'd sure like to know. Certainly pornography wouldn't be one of the country's major businesses if people were doing it instead of watching it. Major league sports have made the entire nation into onlookers in my opinion. They don't think they should be doing it. They think they should be watching it. So count yourself lucky that you're gay. At least when the fire has burned out between a gay couple, they end it. The Country Club, the mortgage, the children's school aren't holding their relationship in place.

Many gay men now have the idea in their heads that the only way to be happy is to be in a permanent relationship. This is not necessarily true. Do you really want a marriage like your parents had? That isn't your revenge, it's theirs.

Here are some points in which I believe:

1. If you have not had a relationship with someone you love/loved

which was sexually fulfilling, you have not really been alive in this swift passage of the years.

2. For gay men, this is much more likely to occur in a homosexual relationship than in a conventional heterosexual marriage because the two of you are not trying to conform. You are not there to fulfill your parents and society's wishes for you. You are there because you want to be together and you are defying society rather than conforming to it. You are much more likely to have good sex and good love.

3. You can call it marriage, you can call it a relationship, you can call it a romance or an affair. All that stuff is just names for a thing, which is the wish of two people to be together. So call it whatever you like.

The sexual wrap-up

It is this writer's conviction that everyone, gay or not, is searching for a fulfilling life so that when they lay down to die they can say to themselves, "There I had it, I saw it, I lived it, I'm quite willing to go."

Sexual fulfillment, however brief, however difficult, is a must.

None of us, and gay men particularly, are here to be little cogs in the smoothly rolling machine of society and culture. We are each an emissary from somewhere else, trying to really live. Not fitting in, being rejected, not being rich and powerful, all that can be disappointing but it has nothing to do with our being here. Life is all about you. It is not about what they think of you. Get that straight.

Only involve yourself with someone who shares your love and sex. You can rise above bad table manners and a poor vocabulary. You cannot rise above being with someone with whom you really don't want to have sex. This is important information. Don't forget it.

Love

Love is placing someone else's welfare before your own.
This can apply to your lover, your parents, children and pets. You do not really love someone if they don't come first.

In every love relationship there is the lover and the loved one.
Even if it balances out 51% and 49%, one of the two parties is giving more, the other is receiving more. It is always better to be the lover than the loved one. Because even if it works out badly, you are the one who has had the experience. You are the one who has felt something. The one who has loved. The loved one only has the feeling of being guilty for not loving as much.

Do not complain if you feel you love your partner more than he loves you. In every relationship this is inevitable. There is nothing unusual or irregular about it. On the other hand, Quentin Crisp once told me that if you have loved greatly, it's only fair that you take your turn in the barrel and allow someone to love you. A person experienced in love can do this and appreciate the experience.

Is there any real difference between lust and love? I think it is very much the same thing. To love someone who does not arouse you sexually is a losing game. If a relationship turns sour, at least you know why you are there. You were crazy about them. If you were never crazy about them then you really have no excuse to be there.

Love always involves being infatuated with someone who fits an idea you already have in your head. You become unhappy with them to the degree that their reality comes into conflict with your fantasy. Understand this. Appreciate them for those qualities that allow you to live your fantasy. Forgive them for their reality that doesn't fit.

Being in love with someone has its time limits. Hopefully the two of you will like being together a lot by the time it runs out.

And you can go on, enjoying the memory of the romance you once had. In Proust's "Remembrance of Things Past" the central character Swann marries his mistress Odile when he no longer is in love with her. He could never marry her while he was very much in love because he knew jealousy would drive him crazy. But once he could see her clearly as a superficial, pretty woman who could love no one he married her, as a kind of memorial to the great love of his life. He knew he would never wish to experience it again. And he would live on with his memory of that great experience. That's not a bad way to think about love.

Another way of thinking about it is this. Love is like an airplane voyage. Once launched and in the air everything is simpler, more focused. The lovers are upon a trajectory and love is their only concern. But finally the need for fuel and the impossibility of continued simplicity requires that there be a landing. One must return to earth. And as records show, most crashes occur upon landing.

A word about choosing a lover and falling in love in the homosexual world. I think there is a direct relationship between the glittering and available presentation of male beauty and the amount of baggage concealed behind that beauty. Those lost and lonely and burned-out souls somehow automatically create a façade of bravado and sexual expertise to lure in the unwary. If your new love interest has had many affairs, he may well be a love trap. You have been warned.

How to read men

1. Look at their mouths. Eyes learn to lie very easily, but mouths will tell you the whole truth. If he has narrow little lips and a mouth like a zipped purse, he is not going to give. He may say he will love you but he won't. Everything that he

has is going to be kept for himself. I have seen men with full, sensuous mouths at twenty who by fifty only had the zipped lip. These are non-givers. Beware.

2. Watch him walking away. Men learn to fake it when they approach you. The walk can be athletic and manly. But watch him as he walks away. Does he have the slightly bow-legged walk of a baby with sore feet? Does he seem a little unsteady and heavier than he looks from the front? Is his head bowed a little? You've got a big baby on your hands and it's not going to get any better.

3. Does he slump? Bad posture tells you everything. This is someone who feels the world is weighing on him greatly. He will complain a lot. And complaining is always the province of those who feel helpless. The more helpless they feel the more they complain. This is not a go-get-em guy. But perhaps you prefer that. He could be very dependent upon you.

4. Does he have small hands? I have no theories; I just think something is wrong.

Some advice from people who knew what they were talking about:
1. The writer Margaret Anderson, an early outspoken lesbian, said that if things are not going well with your lover, "Leave and come back as an attractive stranger." A perfect example of returning as a fantasy after the reality of yourself has become too apparent.

2. The famous decorator Elsie DeWolfe, later Lady Mendl, said "Never complain. Never explain." Such excellent advice, again allowing you to remain a fantasy rather than a talkative person about the house. Your lover doesn't want the facts, he wants the fiction.

In the matter of love, no one owes anyone anything. Particularly regular sexual attention. If you want sex, my dear, you must inspire it.

Love and sex

If you really place another person's welfare before your own and they are your lover, then you are concerned whether they are having a good time in bed with you. Not only whether you are having a good time.

If your sex partner is only a fantasy figure or a symbol of masculinity, of course you aren't interested in whether they are having good sex with you or not. For you, they are not really alive. They are just one step past one of those blow-up plastic dolls.

Your dream lover

Gay men probably have no more of a problem with falling in love with fantasies than does the average high school cheerleader. But you should get over it. Those fantasies that are fed to us in the form of Brad Pitt or Taylor Lautner have to do with our genes being irresistibly attracted to the person who is our opposite. The philosopher Nietzsche wrote about it, saying that genes know that breeding with our direct opposite creates the strongest offspring. He didn't point out that it also leaves everyone with a partner who has no shared interests. Homosexuals have the same genetic attraction to those old-fashioned figures of big muscles and strong profiles. But after a couple of turns around the park you really should learn something.

Too many men put themselves together in big muscles and tight clothing to represent the sex symbol other gay men are looking for. But when they get together, what have they got? The same person, pretending to be someone else. It's okay for kids. But a mature person must present himself as he actually is if anyone who really wants him is to find him.

So get this clear. A dream lover can only be a dream. And you need to get real if you are going to find sexual fulfillment. And if you can only have sex with a dream, changing the dream over and over and over, you are in mucho trouble. You have a big battle ahead of you tracking down reality.

On falling in love with straight men

a. On the positive side, nobody is that straight. And everybody loves having someone falling in love with them.

b. On the negative side, are you selling yourself on impossible dreams, just so you don't have to really feel?

And one last word on the subject: Businessmen are lousy lovers

Some small rules once you're in a relationship:

1. Do not say or do anything that diminishes others. Never leave someone feeling less good about themselves because of something you've said.

2. Don't be afraid of being selfish, however. It's just a hair away from self-confidence.

3. Never tell a joke for more than two years.

4. Remember that Tolstoy said, "Anyone who does not want to be lonely should never marry." Do not demand constant attention.

And finally, it's all about intimacy. No matter how big or small the house, rich or poor your lover, good or bad your job, none of this figures in the long run. If you have intimacy with your lover/partner where you feel closer than with anyone else, thatis what it is all about. If you feel it's the two of you against the world, count yourself lucky. And don't underestimate how important it is.

Pedophilia— Forget It!

This is such a difficult subject to discuss, because it is disruptive among gays. I have quizzed many friends about this, and this is where it nets out:

1. Remember yourself as a teenager. If you remember honestly, you'll recall that once those hormones started raging, you were ready for sex. And were probably having plenty with teen friends. Would you have wanted sex with adult males? Did you have sex with adult males? How did you feel about it?

2. The Greeks had a word for it. Ancient Greek culture had an accepted and established practice of older men loving younger men. The younger men were in a period of late adolescent beauty. They were certainly not children. Both boys and girls were considered at their most beautiful at this flowering before adulthood. Girls and women were destined only for the home, so boys became the object of desire for men. Sex between two older males was taboo. There were also no tops and bottoms in this world (suppos-

edly.) Older men reached orgasm between the thighs of their young male friends.

What the young friends did seems to never be discussed. Certainly more went on than is classically discussed. The point being, that what is now illegal was once a lifestyle.

3. Never impose on others. There is nothing worse than having sex when you don't feel like it. This is true of anyone, anywhere, anytime. Many men don't seem to be concerned whether their partner feel like it. This is a huge mistake. If you are involved with a young man, not a child, who clearly is interested in having sex I leave it to you as to what you plan to do. I also leave the legal ramifications in your hands.

4. Children never. A child has no clear idea of what sex means or involves. The child may not wish to displease you but the child is not seriously interested in having sex with you. You shouldn't kid yourself about this. Your interests can be very harmful to others. See someone about this. You need to grow up.

How to Dress

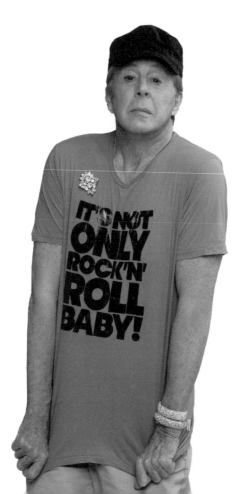

If you must have a female role model, may I recommend Katherine Hepburn or Angelina Jolie: lots of pants, lots of attitude, no jewelry. Please, not Madonna. And certainly not Lady Gaga. No one wants to come home to that.

Dress plain

You don't have to dress to look particularly masculine. But if you're not sure what looks good on you, don't wear a lot of stuff. You can never go wrong with a tee-shirt, blue jeans and a very expensive blazer.

Good shoes

You've heard this forever but it's true. You can run around in a tee-shirt and jeans, a cheap white shirt and black pants, what have you, but one glance at your shoes tells any knowledgeable person whether you have taste or not. They should be leather, brown and plain. And please do not wear sneakers all the time. You're a big boy now.

No fur coats

In the fashion business, the adage is, "Furs add ten years to anyone's age." That great fashion goddess Babe Paley never wore fur. This is not about animals. This is about you.

Tight clothes do not make for tight relationships

Isn't the short shorts and tank top a little bit like the big-breasted girl in the pink angora sweater? A little desperate. Being cool doesn't mean wearing skimpy clothes.

Do not wear inappropriate shorts

That is, above your knees. Get rid of the shorts of your youth.

Jewelry

1. If you're not sure avoid it. Neck chains are extremely questionable, unless you're wearing a big silver one with black, which suggests that you either would like to beat someone up or be beaten up by them.

2. If you are going to wear jewelry, wear big. Small jewelry tells too much about you. Little rings, little wrist chains, make you look rinky-dink. A big watch, a big wrist chain, a great big ring and even a great big brooch on your lapel can be fine. No one will know exactly what you're up to except that you are daring.

Drag—
Is It a Good Idea?

One of my most serious disagreements with drag is that it makes fun of homosexuality. I think homosexuality is not something to be ridiculed. You don't see women putting themselves together in an exaggerated way to make fun of their own sex. I think homosexuals owe each other the same kind of respect.

In the American Indian culture there were some men who chose to dress as women, do women's work and live with a man. They were called "berdache." They were considered some kind of magical representation of the will of an all-powerful being and always well respected. This is fine and much to be respected. So if you feel you must put yourself together as a woman, don't make fun of yourself doing it.

Quentin Crisp once told me that he thought it strange that when men put themselves together to look like women they always dressed as whores and when women put themselves together to look like men they always dressed as truck drivers. There is something to think about here if you have a drive to represent yourself as another kind of outcast, or at best a kind of clown.

I have always believed that if a man wants a woman, there are plenty of real ones around. Recently I have learned otherwise. There are men who actually are excited by drag queens, but as one man told me, "But definitely pre-op. When you get down there you do want a cock." Well, maybe your problem and his problem can come up with a solution. Good luck.

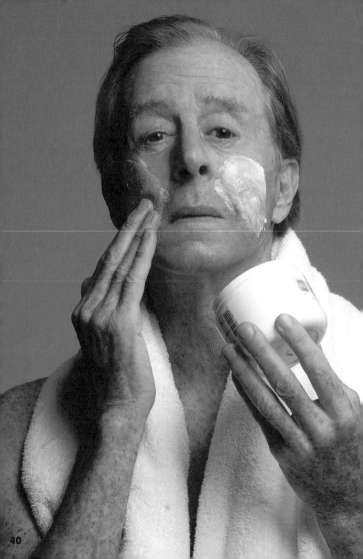

Beauty, Beauty, Beauty

And now for the chapter on beauty. And don't say that it is not important. Please. The world revolves around two things: beauty and money. Both are a search for power. And why do we search for power? So as to control everything so nothing can go wrong. And what are the people like who have the power to pretty much control everything in their lives? Bored. And boring. But this is not for you. You are above all that. You love beauty for beauty's sake, don't you? Of course you do. Particularly your own.

You owe it to your public to remain fuckable

Do not believe for one moment that the person (or persons) who love you don't care if you've gained weight. If they truly don't it's because they don't care about sleeping with you anymore either. Blame it on genetic structure, but our genes force us to want to make bamboola with attractive people, the most likely prospects in the gene pool. And as one wise photographer counseled me once about a lover, "If he's not sleeping with you he's sleeping with somebody." Your physical appearance is just one of the tools in keeping your relationship and your life together.

Everyone is beautiful at their best. I know the story you're going to give me. That you've never been thin. That you've always been skinny (lucky you). That you're getting bald. You're bow-legged, knock- kneed, whatever. Then I want to hear that you are doing everything you can to look good. Are you avoiding junk food, are you standing up straight, are you going to the gym regularly, are you clean? All these things are crucial. And as I say repetitively in this book, if you aren't doing your best to have love and a relationship in your life, perhaps you don't really want it.

You are always somebody's type
It's true. Young or old, chubby or slender, flowing locks or bald, there will always be someone to fancy you. Whether you fancy them is another story. But if you are not appearing before the eyes of the world at your best, you're not giving yourself a fair shake.

Do you want to be loved by somebody or everybody?
If you are one of those "everybody" people you will want to have muscles, at this moment in time. Be honest. If this what you really want, go for it. Get a regular gym routine and work like hell. Don't forget to do your legs, too. You'll want to wear shorts sometimes.

But be prepared, the lissome slender body is heading our way again as a desireable type, as you will see in the fashion magazines. This was the ideal in the Fifties, Sixties and Seventies (Mick Jagger, The Beatles, Steve McQueen, even Warren Beatty in "Shampoo.") Don't go so far you can't shed all those pecs and biceps if you want to.

Your body
Keep your weight under control, keep scrupulously clean, wear simple clothes. It's really enough.

Fat
1. Buy five pounds of hamburger. Open the package and look at. Imagine it on your body. Five pounds is enormous. Think of that pile of hamburger every time you are about to order a dessert or butter up another piece of bread.

2. Do you think cold food has fewer calories than hot? Do you think food you eat standing up doesn't count? Do you think food you eat from someone else's plate doesn't count? Wrong.

3. Do you eat because it's mealtime? Wrong. You don't have to ever eat if you don't want to. If you don't feel like it don't do it. Have an iced tea instead.

4. How about only eating half your meal? Your mother isn't present to force you to finish your plate (hopefully). If you only eat half of what is on your plate you'd be amazed how that flesh fades away.

5. Lastly, are you wrapping your sexual organs in fat rolls so they don't have to function? So no one can get at them? I happen to think fat is very much involved with fear of sex. Think about this. You may have more work to do than just avoiding doughnuts.

Hair

There is absolutely nothing wrong with not having hair. What's wrong are all those cover-ups:

1. The comb-over. Do we even have to discuss this?

2. Hair transplants. Have there ever been any that don't look like some kind of mini-plant is growing out of your head? If so, be my guest.

3. The toupee. I was making out with someone once who said, "Please don't touch my hair." I immediately didn't want to touch anything. No use looking nice if you can't be touched.

Lots of testosterone makes you lose your hair. Everybody knows that. Balding guys are the sexiest and the cognoscenti are well aware of this.

To keep your hair in your head, however, try these things:

1. Stand on your head every morning. The layer of skin over the top of your skull is the thinnest on your body. As you get older it is increasingly difficult for your heart to pump blood through these veins, which carry the blood that nourishes the roots of your hair. So hair dies and falls out. If you stand on your head blood gets down there and hair doesn't have to go on a famine diet.

2. Massaging the head, neck and shoulders is important too, to get that blood up there. You can get one of those massage units to attach to your hand that works great. It does not particularly work well elsewhere, so forget about it.

3. Be sure your scalp is very clean. It produces a lot of oil that can clog the roots. And pimples on your scalp, even if invisible, can do damage.

Sleep

1. Sleep. Need I repeat? Sleep and sleep and more sleep. If you have trouble sleeping, remember it doesn't matter if you are really

asleep as long as you are lying flat on your back with your eyes closed in a darkened room. This was my mother's theory and it sent her insomniac children to sleep like a whiz. Her other advice, "Sleep on your back and don't press your face into the pillow. It makes wrinkles."

2. Facials. Don't sneer. Keeping your facial skin clean and relaxed is very important.

You can give yourself one. I recommend Mario Badesco products. Tighten. Reduce spots and redness. Or go get one. They really improve your skin.

3. Skin care. You're sneering again. Please don't. I haven't washed my face since I was thirty. And I don't care how drunk I am when I come home. I always cleanse, tone and put on night cream. No soap and water. You don't think this is very masculine? It isn't. We're talking beauty here. And you did buy this book. And you have read this far.

My final advice:
Think of yourself as a great beauty Your self-presentation in public should be that of someone who is used to being looked at, not one of those onlookers.

1.Never turn to look at another man in the street. Even if you friends are going ooh! And aah! And grabbing your arm.

2. Have good posture. Walk, stand and sit as though you are expecting to be photographed. If you do this you won't be one of the gang. Great beauties are not one of the gang.

3. Expect to be admired. We do not get what we hope for, we get what we expect.

4. You do not have to be especially vivacious or talkative or peppy Leave that for the short ones. Be there but be a star.

5. Always leave as though you are going somewhere more interesting.

Dark glasses

Always make sure they are big enough and dark enough. So you can avoid squinting and making wrinkles. Jacqueline Kennedy Onassis knew what she was doing with her big Gucci sunglasses.

Blonds

There are only two real pieces of advice for those who are blond.

Ignore brunette criticism
The idea that blonds are frigid is just a lot of brunette gossip.

As they get older, blonds should go south
When you are no longer getting the attention you want (or expect) in New York try moving to Miami Beach. And after Miami Beach begins to lose interest you can try Mexico. I myself live part of the year in Montevideo, Uruguay. The men are very handsome there.

And finally you can go to Tierra del Fuego, the jumping off point for Antarctica. I was there last year. They were crazy about me.

On Getting Older

This will not be a chapter on adjusting mentally to getting older. There is no such thing. Nor will there be any discussion of the joys of being older. That seems highly conjectural. This is primarily about how to seem younger. With some pointers about how you can change your attitudes somewhat about things sexual.

Remember this:
You can always look ten years younger than you are
This was a Babe Paley dictum, but she added, "Do not hope to look more. Ten is the maximum." And she knew what she was talking about.

Here is how you do it
1. Sleep. Sleep and sleep and sleep, my darlings. I usually sleep nine hours a night and could easily sleep more. On the week ends I always stay in bed until noon on Saturday and Sunday. Your brain doesn't actually need to rest. Did you know that? The more your body rests the better you look.

2. Don't smoke. Who the hell cares about your lungs? Tobacco smoking lines your face terribly.

Need I say more. If you must smoke try to only do it in public where you can throw your vices into the face of public opinion.

3. Must you drink? You really should try not to drink. It ruins your looks. The trouble with alcohol is that it makes you feel young and look old. The reverse is a much preferable situation: feel old and look young. Every time I look in the mirror I'm amazed; I feel like I should look one hundred.

4. Don't worry about your emotions. My personal experience is that the worse you feel the better you look. And that's a deal I'm willing to make. My mother (I promise she's not coming up anymore) also said that at least when you had a lot of worries you got thin. Bless her. It was just an echo of Marilyn Monroe, who when asked if she was happy replied, "Let's just say that I'm thin." Exactly. First things first.

5. Be as thin as you can. Coco Chanel said,"After a certain age you must choose between your face and your ass." I think you must always choose your ass. Things can be done about your face.

6. Exercise, Exercise, Exercise. This is crucial. And I don't mean

long walks. Even swimming really doesn't burn many calories. Go to the gym. It will keep you good-looking and strong for the very long run.

7. Your face. Well, here we go. You must cleanse, tone and moisturize and use night cream. I have already discussed this. You shriek and throw your hands in air. Such sissy stuff: All right, get all dried out like an old prune and see who cares.

Your face and hands are exposed to the elements constantly. They need to be protected. Go to a good beauty-oriented dermatologist like Mario Badescu in New York and do what they tell you to do. You will see all the great models of the past there like Patty Hanson and they all look great. Just do what they tell you to do and stick with it. Spend your money on your face; it's far more important than jewelry or clothes.

8. Plastic surgery. Do not be gun-shy. Finally there's nothing that can be done about your neck when it goes. Remember, always moisturize your neck. Someday it may be your face. And then one day, it must be pulled up. Start there. And maybe your eyes should be done, too. Don't go for a full facelift all at once.

Forget about having your nose done or implants. They are silly and only change you for the worse. Your goal is to keep looking the way you did between 45 and 50.

Don't have any doctor touch you unless he's already worked on one of your friends and the results are good. Do not look for tight, tight, tight. You don't want to wind up looking like Joan Rivers.

9. Stand on your head. It is so beneficial. Keeps the hair in your head by keeping the blood circulating through that thin stretch of scalp that underlies your haircut. Also excellent for letting your organs take a break from the pull of gravity.

10. Dress down. As you get older do not put more stuff on. Coco Chanel (finally, she said everything) said, "Stand in front of the mirror before you go out and take off one thing." It could certainly be your neck chain.

Just wear navy blue, white, beige and black. Occasionally wear pink just to keep them on their toes. But always have a light color near your face. Preferably white. And be clean. Do you hear me, clean, clean, clean!

If you live in a shoe and sock wearing world, be sure your socks come up high enough. The shin is really sad looking if you're not tan.

If you are in a sunny climate, use gallons of body lotion. Make sure your legs and arms never look dry.

11. The sun. I personally am rather for the sun. But be judicious. Go out after three o'clock and bask for about an hour. You will build up a nice, ruddy look. Do not dream that by baking for hours and hours you're covering up your wrinkles. You will not only look old you will look like an old alligator purse.

Okay, now assuming that you look damn good and are definitely still fuckable, let's talk about relations. Who was it said, "Of all my relations, I like my sexual ones the best."? Precisely. What everyone is concerned with, men and women, is having a romantic relationship that includes hanky-panky as they get older. Some things to consider:

1. Older Man/Younger man. We've all seen it. Wealthy older man. Cute younger man. Older man is convinced that younger man loves him for himself. We see it and smirk at it, but is it any different than an older man and a younger woman? They're making a deal. He gets sex with a young body, the spouse gets security. The only thing missing would seem to be true intimacy. Can you get along without that? Remember, you never see a younger man with a poor older man.

2. Laughable Loves. Please don't be getting crushes on much younger men you can only long for. Only heterosexual men are allowed by society to never grow up. Women and homosexuals must grow up to survive. Impossible and laughable loves only mean you have no real intention of having a true romantic relationship with anyone and you prefer to slip off into the world of dreams. This really isn't worthy of you.

3. The Blow Job. Many older men seem to think giving someone a blowjob constitutes a sex life. I assure you it does not. A blowjob is only just a blowjob. It is just a preliminary to sexual intercourse and has nothing to do with a real

relationship. I think you should hold out for the relationship. Perhaps I'm being too demanding. Perhaps you don't really want one.

4. Pornography. Do not underestimate the necessity of pornography in the older person's life. Even the famous and innovative architect Buckminster Fuller was quoted as saying it was very important in the later years. Truly, "If you don't use it you lose it." If you are ashamed to admit that you masturbate you are truly of another time and space. Everybody does it. And as you get older it's a must. And, as the line from the "The Boys in the Band" goes, "It doesn't matter how your hair looks."

5. On Embarrassing Yourself. Always keep firmly in mind what you used to think about older men. The toupees, the comb-overs, the obvious dye job, the paid hustlers, the inappropriate lover or boyfriend, the desperation. Don't embarrass yourself, don't kid yourself. As you get older you must get tougher and tougher with yourself.

6. On Loneliness. Just because you're not with someone doesn't mean you're doomed to loneliness. Many couples are individually lonely. In both heterosexual and homosexual couples, how many of them have a best friend who is not the person they're living with? Ideally, if you are with someone they are not only your love object but also your best friend. To avoid loneliness, try this:

7. Think of Others. The minute you feel lonely think of someone who may be lonelier than yourself. It is not necessarily another man. It could be an older person, a younger person on their own, etc. It should probably not be someone who is a possibility as a relationship. Then there is no hidden agenda. You'll be amazed how quickly loneliness dissipates the moment you concern yourself with someone else who needs your attention.

8. Hang Around With Younger People. Nothing is more aging than being with your own age group. Those gray-haired outsiders, all at a table together goggling at young passers-by. Unflattering image. Being with older people you start walking carefully, lowering yourself into chairs, peering through bifocals. Stay with younger people and you won't start acting this way. Immediately you will say, "But how?"

Make an effort, my dear. Give parties. Have a gym trainer you really like (please don't fall in love with him) and get to know his friends. Invite him and his pals to the movies. If you act like them they will not think of you as an older person.

9. Slumping. There is absolutely no need for this. You think this is how people behave at your age so you do it. Please don't. There is absolutely no need to pick up this kind of behavior from your peers.

10. Join Things. Get into local gay activities. If there's a Gay Men's Chorus, join it. Even if you can't sing. That doesn't matter. Any Gay and Lesbian organization is good, too. These are the local energetic young folks of your community. They need your help. They don't particularly need your money but they can certainly use a mature point of view on many things.

11. Get to Know Your Neighbors. Young couples, young non-gay men and women all like having a more mature person among their friends. Many lack any real decent parenting (heterosexual older couples are the worst) and just make sure you are really making friends

and being a friend. Using friendship as a guise for finding a lover never works. But you'll be surprised how attractive your ever-youthful demeanor is to others you would never suspect might become interested in you. This is really good advice. Take it.

Older style

Avoid the Jewish Mother syndrome. Never make younger people feel it is their duty to see you and spend time with you. Always be doing more interesting things than they are.

Tell them, "I can't be with you at Thanksgiving. I'm visiting a friend on the Isle of Lesbos." This is an ideal example of how to make younger people want to know you. Of course you must truly have a friend on the Isle of Lesbos. This part is up to you.

Your Job

For myself, I am only capable of about an hour and a half of meaningful living per day. I can only muster intense feelings for that amount of time and that leaves another 22 1/2 hours to fill. You eat, you sleep, and there's still plenty of time to work eight hours a day. And since you have the time you might as well fill it by earning a living.

There are two reasons to have a job:

1. You are doing something very meaningful that fills you with joy and it doesn't matter that that you're not making much money because the money is only for you to enjoy your life, and you're already enjoying your life. This is a small category filled with people like Pablo Picasso. We can not all be with Dr. Schweitzer in Africa saving the natives. The meaningful job is not all that easy to find and perhaps you are not meant for that.

2. You are working to get the money to pay for your lifestyle. The bulk of us fall into this category. You will be well paid for doing what you

do well, whether you like doing it or not. So enjoy the fact that people truly want you to do what you're doing.

As for the lifestyle you then pay for, that is the hard part. Just following the herd in pursuing sex, food and flashy cars may not be all that satisfying. You will have to find out who you really are and then style a life for yourself. And finding a life partner is not the solution. You will then have to find a lifestyle that suits both of you. Perhaps you should find a lifestyle first, and that will narrow down the partner possibilities.

One last piece of advice!
Better looking people get better jobs. Research has proven this. But please, don't grouse about how unfair it all is. Life is unfair, haven't you noticed? You are here to fight back against the unfairness in a reasonable way.

Money

Some ideas about money

1. Don't turn your nose up at it. You'd be amazed at how many problems go away when you throw money at them. This is your prime reason for working.

2. Avarice. One of the Seven Deadly Sins. Money is not an end in itself, and if you think having money will make you more attractive to other men, you're right. It will. But only to a kind of man whom you are paying for, whether for one night or many years. Can you really feel good about yourself knowing that you're paying for it?

3. Stuff. It is true that if you are not able to have the kind of emotional fulfillment you wish through an attachment there can be a kind of fulfillment through art, furniture, jewels and other odds and ends. You will need money for this. But you should always be willing to throw it all over for some man. He may be willing to buy you stuff but what is more important is that he cares about you.

4. Tightwads. On the other hand, a man who is not willing to spend money on you is not willing to give you love either. In my experience this has always proven to be true. Once when starting a relationship with an older man I said to my sister, "He has a lot of money but he never spends it on me and it just isn't right." She replied, "It wouldn't be right even if he didn't have a lot of money." No wonder I loved her.

Your Home

Your home says everything about the state of your inner being. If it is well organized, beautiful to look at, restful and comfortable, you probably are too, inside. This is a good clue also when you see someone else's home.

If their home is awash with unsorted stuff, unwashed laundry and ill-chosen furniture you know this is exactly what this person's interior world is. They cannot put things in order, cannot make decisions, are undisciplined and untenacious. Of course, order and discipline may be what you are bringing to the party. This guy could be your type.

Couples need to complement one another. Perhaps this feckless person with their untrammeled emotion is exactly what you're looking for. You can pick up after him and he can set you free from your neatnik routine.

Beware of decorated homes. You have no idea who this person

is. These large spaces designed for entertaining do not make for a comfortable home. Only for a busy social life.

As for your own taste, you are entitled to whatever you like. Just know what you like. The great fashion editor Diana Vreeland said, "I don't mind bad taste. It's no taste that I don't like."

As long as your home is an expression of you, you're fine. It's when you don't know who the hell you are that your digs begin to look like the perennial grad student's room. You cannot remain a grad student forever. Or perhaps you can. Many people I know seem to be doing it.

Don't wait until you have a partner to start creating a home. Many people will be drawn to you because they like your home and sense immediately what it would be like to be with you all the time.

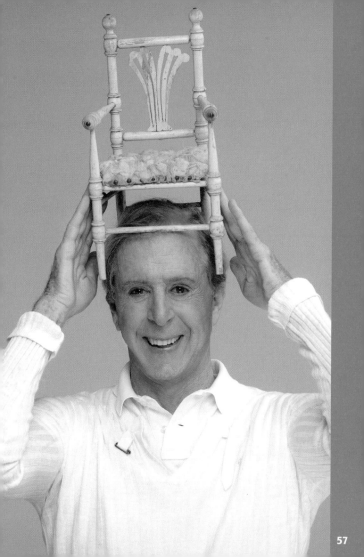

Your Dreams

Please keep turning your dreams in for new ones. If you can't get off the dime because what you dream of is being rich, being famous and being happy with a handsome man, perhaps you should try to personalize where you think you're going.

True, television commercials *still* present images of a happy domestic life that never did exist. Do you truly think your childhood and family life was so different from everyone else's? That is reality. The ups and downs, the backs and forths, the hithers and yons. Try to make your dreams something that is truly accomplishable in terms of your own experience. Then you have some chance of accomplishing them.

Dream of living in Paris? You can do it. Just remember it's cold and gray a lot of the time.

Dream of writing a book? Write just one page a day and you'll have one in less than a year. Don't worry if it doesn't make sense. Once you have 250 pages you can reorganize it.

Dream of being taller? Wear cowboy boots.

Pursue your realistic dreams. You may not get there but you will get somewhere very interesting.

Friendship

Here are the rules for deciding if someone actually figures in your life and is a friend:

1. If they don't see or hear from you in one day, they check to see if you're all right.
2. If they don't see or hear from you in a week, they check to see if you're all right.
3. If they don't see or hear from you in a month, they check to see if you're all right.

If there are people in your life who let a month go by and don't know what you're up to they cannot truly be said to figure in your life. They would not truly miss you.

I have people in my life who would not know if I was dead for six months or a year. They perhaps consider themselves my friends. I do not consider myself theirs.

After Oscar Wilde's disgrace he was walking in a park with an acquaintance who said, "But after all, Oscar, you have so many friends who have stayed loyal to you." Oscar replied," I don't need any more friends. I need a lover." This is shocking in its frankness. But something to mull over. You may just be not doing the necessary work on having an intimate relationship with a partner.

Sitting around in bars chatting with other people also does not constitute friendship. Try getting sick and see how many of them come to see you in the hospital. None is my guess.

If you live in a world where you only have friends who can do something for you or for whom you can do something, you're in trouble.

People who are friendly to you because you can put work in their way (those of you who are in the fashion world know what I mean) also do not constitute friends. Nor should you consider those whom you are cultivating in order to get work to be friends either.

There are only three reasons for knowing somebody:

1. They are beautiful
2. They are interesting
3. They are good

There is no reason to know someone or consider them a friend if they are not in this category. And how about yourself? How do you fit into these categories?

If you are not beautiful and you cannot manage to be interesting, I would highly recommend that you be good.

Breaking Up Is Hard to Do

A plus about gay relationships is that two men are less likely to stay together once their relationship is dead. Heterosexuals stay together because of the kids, the country club, the house, the relatives. But for gay men, when it's over they're out of there. I explained this to a heterosexual married male friend who said, "I know.

I know. There's a lot to be said for homosexual lifestyle. It's only the sex part that I boggle at." Which is to say:

There's no use whipping a dead horse. If the two of you really don't want to sleep together anymore, don't want to talk together anymore, don't want to be together anymore, then split.

Two big hang-ups:

1. One of you wants to stay and the other wants to leave. If you are one of those who doesn't want the relationship to end, let him go gracefully, anyway.

Hopefully you're not involved with joint property ownership. Hopefully you haven't given up everything (including a promising career on the stage) for him. You probably did, and more the fool you.

2. You both are afraid of being alone. This is a fear to conquer. You don't want to replicate heterosexual marriages. My definition of many heterosexual marriages is that you are with someone you don't particularly care about which makes it impossible for you to meet someone you might care about.

Men are not for security, they are for the experience.

If you are being left behind, you're probably the one who loved the most. So you can tell yourself, *the relationship may not have been successful but the experience was.*

If the experience wasn't great and fulfilling, you shouldn't be feeling so bad. If it was, remember, you were the one that got the greatness from the relationship. He missed out.

You have a destiny. Don't fight it. If you consistently do those things you *feel* you should do instead of those things that seem *the sensible* thing to do, you are following your destiny. And that goes well beyond what's right and what's wrong.

You do not always know what is right for yourself. What you want may not be what is right for you and where your destiny is taking you. Frequently we want what our mother wanted, without even thinking that we may have a more singular destiny than she did. Give yourself over to it. Go ahead, suffer. When you suffer you can learn. And that's what this whole process is all about. Learning so as to not make the same mistakes all over again.

Do you wind up with the same sort of guy over and over, always with bad results? This is really something to think about. Not that you should change your type. But realize that the right kind of guy for you basically can not be long lasting. You just want to have that emotional thrill and then it's over. Eventually you will be over the thrill and move on. But don't force yourself. Maybe you will grow up and stay with him.

Finally, do you want a romance or a marriage?

Think seriously about this. If you are in it for romance, this is a terminal activity. It has an end. And then you start again. If you are confusing the two, separate them and ask yourself which one you really prefer. Then do it.

And do you really want to be married? Why in heaven's name would you want a marriage like your parents? Or are you one of those people who think, "Somebody has to get it right?"

Love is like the child of your relationship. When you break up, love dies, and it is exactly like losing a child. So you must suffer. And if you are any kind of person at all you will really never get over it. But life must go on. One of my friends once said to me:

"We've been through some terrible times but we always looked good and we were always fun to be with." This must be your motto. Gay guys and geisha girls have a lot in common. It is not part of our lifescape to be mooning around and looking bad and telling people how terrible we feel. Keep it to yourself. You will get the most out of your suffering that way. Rat-a-tatting about it over the telephone to your friends all the time is very high school. You're only cheapening the experience. And the final piece of knowledge you should have is:

Nothing is over forever until you are both dead.

They do keep coming back, remembering you as the one who really loved them and was their most meaningful relationship. This requires that you look eternally good and remain fun to be with. Can you do it? Hopefully you can.

To Bar or Not to Bar

As for myself:

1. I will go to a gay bar with friends to have fun. I will not go to make new friends.

The music is too loud and the lights are too low.

2. I, personally, don't want to sleep with someone who has had sex with half the

Eastern Seaboard.

3. Also, I go nowhere where being witty and charming counts for nothing.

4. Do not wear tank tops. The tank top deserves some extra attention. The people who look good in them usually don't wear them. That's left for those men who for some reason like to expose that saggy part of the torso right under the arms. Not nice.

5. Behave yourself at the urinal. Please no.

6. Think twice when that perfect guy is from out of town.

7. Do not force your number on anybody. You may take his.

8. Do not get drunk. See below.

Alcohol and drugs

All alcohol and drugs are about is letting you step out of the picture and live in a dream that is chemically generated. If you can afford it, why shouldn't you?

But you must remember you are all alone in this dream. There really is no place for someone else since your world doesn't exist in reality.

And of course, alcohol and drugs are a kind of prison. You can only escape with enormous effort once you are stuck in it. But you can escape to the freedom of making your own decisions and finding some sense of security in your own ability to support yourself. The freedom of being attractive to other people. The freedom of putting down a number of pegs to your personal tent so it can't be blown away in the slightest storm.

But this is your decision. Many people seem to live as though their lives will go on for a million years and it really doesn't matter too much what they do from day to day. So they drink and do drugs. Unfortunately this is not true. You're 21, you're 22, you're 40. And there's nothing other people want to hear less than how you've wasted your life. You actually knew, honey, and you made the decision by not making the decision. Over and out.

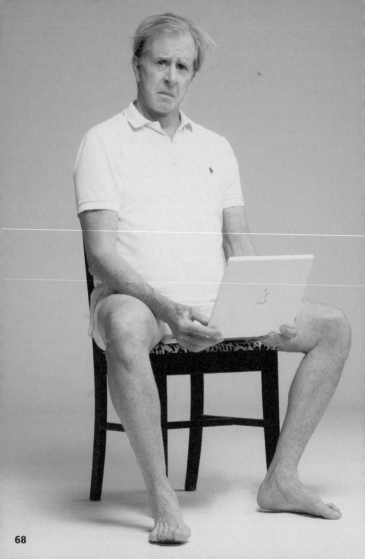

On-line

The internet has greatly increased gay men's opportunities to make contact with other gay men. But has it really made the gay interchange move forward into a more 21st century experience? I think it has moved the possibilities of sex forward enormously. For instance, new developments like Grindr, with which you can actually find out who is sexually available within a few miles, a few minutes from you. But does it make love any easier or any more possible?

Whatever you may think of yourself I believe you are trying to find fulfillment. And fulfillment comes from deeply exploring sex mixed with deeper feelings in a relationship. Having sex with four or five strangers a week may keep you busy but is it really all that different from masturbation?

I know, I know, there are tons of couples who met on the internet. But I still think the overall atmosphere is one of frenetic, almost hysterical activity with people displaying their private parts front and back indiscriminately. Doesn't it look a little desperate to you? Or am I wrong? Maybe you have to step back and take a long look at yourself and the internet. Are you using it just because you are lonely? Honey, you can't be so horny you have to have sex every day. Or maybe you are.

At any rate, the internet is just too easy. Take an evening class in painting. Or ceramics. Or even better, automobile repair. Meet some real people in real situations and ask someone out for coffee. Remember, even the women you meet may have sexy brothers or friends you'll want to know also. And most importantly, remember that you are always somebody's type. You just need a social life. Not a computer

The View Ahead

Take a long look at the century that lies ahead of us. You are in a watershed period where all things are changing so don't labor along with ideas about gayness that will no longer be pertinent in a very few years. Here are some things to think about:

The family is re-shaping. It's really here but we just haven't considered it. In the future we will, define the family in six different ways:

1. Male and female with children who stay together over a long period of time.

2. Male and male or female and female, with or without children who stay together for a long period of time.

3. Single male or single female with child/children.

4. Couple in any kind of combination who stays together as long as their relationship seems meaningful. They then change partners. These are relatively short-term relationships, usually without children. They could be called "affairs." They could be called "Serial Monogamy." This is the kind of relationship many people prefer.

5. A family made up of a number of friends who share a living space. There are generally no sexual relationships among those friends and no children.

6. The one-person family unit. This person lives alone. May or may not have romantic relationships. May have a child or children at some point. Prefers to live this way.

Since all of these lifestyles will be perfectly viable in years ahead, parents will accept any of these as being all right for their child. Therefore the pressure to have a heterosexual long-term marriage will be gone.

Once this pressure is gone, there will be many other more pertinent decisions for gay people to make, the very same ones non-gays have to handle.

1. Do I really want to be rich?

2. Do I really want to be famous?

3. Are the goals the American culture holds up for us spurious?

4. Do we really care what the neighbors think?

5. What should I do to really

have a meaningful and happy life, now it's okay for me to be happy?

Gay men have even more specific questions to ask themselves if they are truly looking for fulfillment. What gay men must remember is that they are after all men, which means:

1. You are competitive.

2. You care very much about how things look, rather than how it feels. Particularly regarding sex.

3. You tend to ignore what you may think of yourself. You prefer to concentrate on what you think of others.

4. You are looking for a caring love but find it difficult to express this kind of care yourself.

All of these things have to be dealt with. Which may mean drawing closer to being like a woman. As women begin to be more like men. The big difference will diminish greatly in this century.

You will not be living a prototypical life.

In the 20th century it was all about leading a life that was supposed to work for everybody. Mom, Dad and the Kids. In this century lives will be individualized. Each person will try to create a life suitable for themselves. This requires knowing who you are. This is not easy.

So as you advance into the 21st Century, be sure you are deploying your energies correctly. Do not waste time worrying about what other people are thinking about you. They aren't. Do not get hung up on fantasies about beautiful men. Work on having a relationship with a real person. But if fantasies are your thing, don't worry about it. You are entitled to be interested in what interests you. Just don't expect your fantasies to overlap with anyone else's reality.

Perhaps the major point of this whole book is that the life that you will have in the future will be very much like everyone else's, gay or not gay. More and more countries are recognizing gay marriages. In more and more countries the traditional marriage and family are falling apart. We are all in this thing together now. Being gay will not be your essential problem. Having a life that suits you will be the solution you are seeking. Just like everyone else. The very best of luck.